SEXUAL PROBLEMS IDENTIFICATION PROFILE

LEWIS DONALD KITE, Ph.D.

GRAPH
Publishing, L.L.C.

Published by
GRAPH Publishing, L.L.C.
www.graphpublishing.com

Printed in the U.S.A.

Table of Contents

ABOUT THE AUTHOR

LEWIS DONALD KITE, Ph.D.

Lewis Donald Kite is the President of Kite Laboratories, Inc. in Houston, Texas. He has formally served as professor of Psychology, NASA subcontractor, and medical laboratory director. At the present, he also provides consulting services to medical professionals in the field of psychiatry.

Dr. Kite received international recognition when he published a paper showing that aspirin is effective in the prevention and treatment of strokes and other vascular disorders. He is a biochemist, mental health professional, medical researcher, and inventor.

Dr. Kite has earned a doctorate in psychology as well as certificates in Art Therapy, Addictionology, Crisis Intervention Stress Management, Hypnotherapy, Neuro-Linguistic Programming, and faith-based counseling. In addition, he has completed six years of postgraduate study in analytical psychology.

Dr. Kite's inventions and tests in medicine and psychology include prescription and non-prescription medications, the Nine Item Symbolic Profile, The Harm Potential Profile, the Sexual Problems Identification Profile, and the Marriage and Family Problems Identification Profile.

Dr. Kite is available for Test Interpretations, Patient Evaluations and Counseling Assistance in regards to Test Results. He may be contacted for hire at the following:

KITE LABORATORIES, Inc.

Dr. Lewis Donald Kite, Ph.D.

Email: ldkite@aol.com

INTRODUCTION

Sigmund Freud would have like to have had this profile to utilize with his patients.

Mental health professionals have been treating the sexual problems of their clients since the days of Sigmund Freud. However, many patients who come for therapy for other issues don't disclose their sexual problems to their therapists. In addition, most people who have been sexually abused won't tell anyone about the abuse and how they feel.

Our Sexual-Problem Identification Profile is designed to aid psychiatrists, other physicians, and licensed mental health professionals in identifying those patients who have been sexually abused and/or have other sexual problems.

The profile was developed after years of study of art therapy, analytical psychology and psychoanalysis. We believe that Sigmund Freud would have liked to have had this profile to utilize with his patients. It is our sincere hope that you will utilize this profile to effectively identify and help sexual abuse victims and others with sexual problems.

The Sexual Problems Identification Profile is an adjunct to the therapeutic process, and is designed to help psychiatrists and other mental health professionals to identify persons who have been sexually abused and others who have sexual problems. This profile provides an insight into the patient's subconscious mind and uncovers problem areas beyond the patient's awareness.

The Profile consists of our Nine-Item Symbolic Profile, a "Draw a Tree" page, and a "Draw a Person" page.

SEXUAL PROBLEMS INDICATED IN THIS PROFILE

1. Voyeurism
2. Fear of castration
3. Problems with masturbation
4. Sexual inadequacy
5. Concern over sexual traits
6. Sexual identification narcissism
7. Exhibitionism
8. Confusion between love and sex
9. Likelihood of affair or expected sexual relations in the future
10. Sexual hang-ups
11. "Sex is wrong" attitude
12. Sexual feelings toward or relationship with the mother
13. Sexual feelings toward or relationship with the father
14. "Playing around" with sex or toying with the idea
15. Sexual assault or sex abuse
16. Abortion or vasectomy
17. Premature sex
18. Infantile sexuality
19. Difficulties in sexual matters
20. Repressed Sexual Desires
21. Insincere affection—coming from the head and not the heart
22. Pain associated with love
23. Death of love in some manner
24. Fear of Sex
25. Fear of past sexual experiences coming to light
26. Anger/hostility connected with love or sex
27. Need for sex but no desire or capacity to give affection

THE NINE-ITEM SYMBOLIC PROFILE

The Nine-Item Symbolic Profile, developed by Dr. Lewis D. Kite, is an adjunct to the therapeutic process. It has been used successfully by mental health professionals to identify patients with sexual problems, as well as other psychological problems. The profile consists of nine symbols that the patient incorporates into a picture that he/she draws. The drawing uncovers sexual problems, other problem areas, and problems in relationships.

Instructions for administering the Nine-Item Symbolic Profile:

Give the patient a copy of the Profile and instruct him/her to draw a picture utilizing all of the symbols listed.

NINE ITEM SYMBOLIC PROFILE

Name _____

Sex _____

Date _____

Age _____

Directions: Draw a picture to include each of the following.

1. House   2. Snake   3. Tree   4. Pond   5. Path   6. Road   7. Fence   8. Person   9. Rainbow

EXAMPLE   NINE ITEM SYMBOLIC PROFILE

Name _____

Sex _____

Date _____

Age _____

Directions: Draw a picture to include each of the following.

1. House   2. Snake   3. Tree   4. Pond   5. Path   6. Road   7. Fence   8. Person   9. Rainbow

"DRAW A PERSON" AND "DRAW A TREE" PAGES

The "Draw a Person" exercise reflects what the subject would like to be, his attitude toward interpersonal relationships, special fears, beliefs, and how he sees himself in the environment. It offers a psychological and physiological overall impression of the subject." (Kouguell, 1994)11

The drawing that a patient makes of a human figure represents the "self" in the environment. The actual presentation of the self may reflect the patient's deepest wishes. It may reflect and expose a painful physical or emotional defect. It may be a vigorous compensation for the defect, or it may reflect a combination of all these factors. (Handler, 1965)7

The tree drawing arouses more subconscious and unconscious associations. It frequently is a projection of the individual's experience and resources. The tree that is drawn also represents the growth, energy level and feeling of interpersonal balance. It is a reflection of a self-portrait. (Buck, 1948)1

INSTRUCTIONS FOR "DRAW A PERSON" AND "DRAW A TREE" PAGES:

1.   Give a copy of the "Draw a Person" page to the patient and instruct him or her to draw a person on the page.

2.   Give a copy of the "Draw a Tree" page to the patient and instruct him/her to draw a tree on the page.

Draw A Person

Name_____   Date_____

Sex_____   Age_____

Directions: Draw a picture of a person.

Draw A Person

Name_____   Date_____

Sex_____   Age_____

Directions: Draw a picture of a tree.

_____

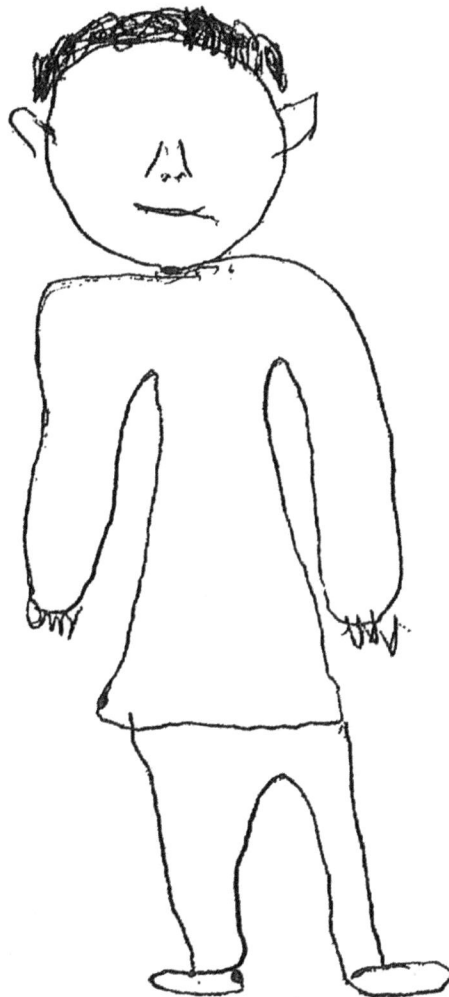

Draw A Tree

Name_____   Date_____

Sex_____   Age_____

Directions: Draw a picture of a tree.

Draw A Tree

Name_____   Date_____

Sex_____   Age_____

Directions: Draw a picture of a tree.

SEXUAL-ABUSE VICTIM IDENTIFICATION CHECK LIST

NINE-ITEM SYMBOLIC PROFILE: (Kite, 1998)10

Check those indicators that appear in the drawing:

_____ 1. A snake in the pond usually indicates some type of sexual abuse. See example #2.

_____ 2. The appearance of a snake in the path indicates sexual feelings or sexual relationship with the mother.

_____ 3. Ducks in the pond indicate some sort of abuse—either sexual or emotional—most often sexual.

_____ 4. Fish in the pond indicates abuse.

_____ 5. A snake coiled up indicates the fear of sex or guilt associated with sex.

_____ 6. A snake hiding in the grass or flowers indicates a fear that past sexual experiences might come to light.

_____ 7. A snake in the pond indicates sexual feelings toward or sexual relationship with the father.

TREE DRAWING:

Check those indicators that appear in the tree drawing.

_____ 8. A hole in the tree in the "Draw a Tree" page and/or on the Nine-Item Symbolic Profile is an indication of sexual abuse. (Kite, 1998)10

_____ 9. A blackened hole in tree indicates shame associated with sexual experience. (Kouguell)11

_____ 10. Pine trees indicate pain associated with love or sex. (Kite, 1998)10

_____ 11. Absence of leaves on a tree, or a dead tree, indicates the need for sex, but no desire or capacity to give affection. (Kite, 1998)10

_____ 12. The presence of heavy lines drawn in the tree indicate anger/hostility connected with love or sex. (Kite, 1998)10

SEXUALLY-ABUSED VICTIM SCALE

Put a check mark beside the number corresponding to those indicators that appear in the drawings.

_____1   _____2   _____3   _____4   _____5   _____6

_____7   _____8   _____9   _____10   _____11   _____12

TOTAL NUMBER OF SEXUAL-ABUSE INDICATORS: _____ out of 12

The more indicators there are, the greater the evidence of sexual abuse.

OTHER INDICATORS OF SEXUAL PROBLEMS IN THE NINE-ITEM SYMBOLIC PROFILE

(Kite, 1998)10

Check those indicators that appear in the drawing.

_____ 1. A snake near the fence is an indication of sexual hang-ups.

_____ 2. A snake on the left side of the drawing indicates that the person thinks that sex is wrong.

_____ 3. A snake in the house is an indication of possible problems with masturbation.

_____ 4. A snake hiding in the grass or flowers indicates a fear that past sexual experiences will come to light.

_____ 5. A snake at the top of the drawing is an indication of the likelihood of sexual fantasies.

_____ 6. A snake at the bottom of the drawing is an indication that sex is foremost In the mind of the client.

_____ 7. A coiled snake indicates some fear of sex, the fear of losing it, or guilt associated with intimacy.

_____ 8. A snake on the right side of the drawing indicates that the person thinks that sex is right.

_____ 9. A snake in the road indicates that sex is important to the client.

_____ 10. A snake near the road indicates the likelihood that the client has had an affair or may have the expectation of a sexual relationship in the future.

_____ 11. A drawing of a person playing with a snake indicates that the client is "playing around" with sex or toying with the idea.

_____12. The presence of fish in the pond is an indication of negative feelings and abuse.

_____13. A drawing with ducks in the pond indicates negative feelings and abuse.

_____14. The appearance of waves in the water of the pond indicates some sort of conflict with the client's father and may indicate a sexual relationship.

_____15. Grass in the drawing can indicate abortion in a woman client and vasectomy in men.

OTHER SEXUAL PROBLEM INDICATORS: IN THE PERSON DRAWING

Check those indicators that appear in the drawing.

_____1. The omission of hair on the person drawn indicates feelings of sexual inadequacy (Buck, 1950)2 and/or fear of castration. (Hammer, 1953)5

_____2. The over-emphasizing of hair indicates concern over sexual traits. (Kouguell) 1994)11

_____3. Facial hair indicates striving for virility and possible feelings of sexual inadequacy. (Kouguell, 1994)11

_____4. Disheveled hair indicates sexual concerns and sexual impassivity. (Kouguell, 1994)11

_____5. Full lips indicate possible issues of sensuality or dependence or sexual identification…may indicate narcissistic tendencies. (Machover, 1949)14

_____6. Protruding lips may indicate aggressive oral tendencies. (Meyer, et al., 1955)16

_____7. The appearance of large eyes in the drawing indicate possible voyeuristic tendencies. (Kouguell, 1994)11

_____8. The omission of eyes indicates possible voyeuristic tendencies. (Kouguell, 1994)11   See example #3.

_____9. A long nose or phallic indicates the possibility of exhibitionism. (Kouguell, 1994)11

_____10. A triangular nose may indicate infantile sexuality. (Urban, 1963)17

_____11.   A nose drawn shaded or truncated indicates a fear of castration. (Hammer, 1953)5 If drawing is done by a female, the indication is of penis envy and hostile feelings toward another. (Machover, 1949)14

_____12.   A mouth pictured as oval or full and open indicates oral-erotic dependencies and possibly difficulties in maintaining cognitive control over bodily drives. (Jolles, 1952)6

_____13.   Omitted fingers indicates possible self-punishment for masturbation tendencies. (Jolles, 1971)9

_____14.   Arms or hands detached from the body indicate a possible fear of castration. (Hammer, 1953)5

_____15.   Feet overemphasized indicates difficulties in sexual matters. (Hammer, 1954)6

_____16.   Omitted feet indicates sexual disturbance (Evans and Marmorston, 1963)3

_____17.   Very broad shoulders indicate possible aggression or uncertainty about sexual matters. (Levy, 1950)4

_____18.   Drawing an overdressed person indicates narcissism or psychological difficulties. (Machover, 1941)13 or repressed sexual drives (Gurvitz, 1951)4 and possible exhibitionist tendencies. (Urban, 1963)17

_____19.   A seductive drawing by a pre-adolescent indicates a possible abnormality (Machover, 1960)14 or may be associated with narcissism. (McElhaney, 1969)15

_____20.   An overdressed or nude figure indicates narcissistic and immature tendencies with psycho-sexual difficulties. (Levy, 1950)12

_____21.   Boots are an indication of concerns over sexual virility. (Kouguell, 1994)11

OTHER SEXUAL PROBLEM INDICATORS: IN THE TREE DRAWING

Check those indicators that appear in the drawing.

_____1. A blackened hole in the tree indicates the presence of shame associated with the sexual experience. (Kouguell, 1994)11

_____2. Knot holes are sexual symbolism indicating abuse, either sexual or emotional. (Kite, 1998)10

_____3. A small, simple knot hole is an indicator of sexual assault in the sexual experience. (Kite, 1998)10

_____ 4. A snake in the tree symbolizes masturbation. (Kite, 1998)10

_____5. A snake near the tree indicates the possibility of uncertainty about the differences between love and sex. (Kite, 1998)10

_____6. Heavy lines drawn on the tree indicates anger and hostility connected to love or sex. (Kite,1998)10

_____7. The absence of leaves indicates a need for affection but no desire or capacity to give affection. (Kite, 1998)10

_____8. A transparent tree reveals that the affection the person gives is not real, coming from the head, not the heart. (Kite, 1998)10

_____9. The presence of pine trees indicate pain associated with love or sex. (Kite, 1998)10

_____10. A drawing of a stump instead of a full tree indicates the death of love in some manner. (Kite, 1998)10

SEXUAL PROBLEMS CHECKLIST

Check those sexual problems indicated on the profile.

_____1. Sexually abused

_____2. Voyeurism

_____3. Fear of castration

_____4. Problems with masturbation

_____5. Sexual inadequacy

_____6. Concern about sexual matters

_____7. Sexual identification

_____8. Exhibitionism

_____9. Confusion between love and sex

_____10. Likelihood of affair or expected sexual relationship in the future

_____11. Sexual hang-ups

_____12. "Sex is wrong" attitude

_____13. Sexual feelings toward or sexual relationship with mother

_____14. Sexual feelings toward or sexual relationship with father

_____15. "Playing around" with or toying with the idea of sex

_____16. Abortion or vasectomy

_____17. Premature sex

_____18. Infantile sexuality

_____19. Difficulties in sexual matters

_____20. Repressed sex drives

_____21. Affection not genuine, coming from the head instead of the heart

_____22. Pain associated with love

_____23. Death of love in some manner

_____24. Fear of sex

_____25. Fear of exposure of past sexual experiences

_____26. Anger/hostility connected with love or sex

_____27. Need for sex but no desire or capacity to give affection

BIBLIOGRAPHY AND REFERENCES

1. Buck, J.M. 1948. "The H-T-P Technique, a Qualitative and Quantitative Scoring Manual."Journal of Clinical Psychology 4: 317-396.

2. Buck, J.M. "Administration & Interpretation of the H-T-P Test:" Proceedings of the H-T-P workshop held at Veterans Administration Hospital, Richmond, Virginia, March 31-April 2, 1950. Lost Angeles: Western Psychological Services, 1950.

3. Evans, R.B. & Marmorston, I. "Psychological Test Signs of Brain Damage in Cerebral Thrombsis." Psychological Reports: 915-930.

4. Gurvitz, M. The Dynamics of Psychological Testing. New York: Grune and Straton,1951.

5. Hammer, E.F. 1953. "An Investigation of Sexual Symbolism: A Study of H-T-P's of Eugenically Sterilized Subjects." Journal of Projective Techniques 17: 401-413.

6. Hammer, E.F. 1954. "An Experimental Study of Symbolism on the Bender Gestalt. Journal of Projective Techniques 18: 335-345.

7. Handler, L. & Reyher, J. 1965. "Figure Drawing Anxiety Indices: A Review of the Literature. Jounal of Projective Techniques 29: 305-313.

8. Jolles, I. A Catalogue for the Quantitative Interpretation of H-T-P. Los Angeles: Western Psychlogical Services,1952.

9. Jolles, I. A Catalogue for the Quantitative Interpretation of H-T-P. Los Angeles: Western Psychological Services, 1952.

10. Kite, L.D. A Guide to Art Therapy. Houston, Texas, 1998.

11. Kouguell, M. DAPTH Assessing the Unconscious in the Practice of Hypnotherapy and Counseling, 1994.

12. Levy, S. 1950. "Figure Drawing as Projective Test." N.L. Abt. & L. Bellak. Eds. Projective Psychology, (New York: Knoff, 1950) 257-297.

13. Machover, K. Personality Projection in the Drawings of the Human Figure. Springfield, Illinois, 1949.

14. Machover, K. "Sex Differences in the Development Pattern of Children Seen in Human Figure Drawings.(A. I Rabin & M. Haworth, eds.) Projective Techniques with Children. (New York: Grune & Stratton), 1060.

15. McElhaney, M. Clinical Psychological Assessment of the Human Figure Drawing. Springfield, Illinois: Thomas. 1969.

16.   Meyer, B.C., Brown, F., Pevine, A. 1955. "Observations on the Human-Tree-Person Drawing Test Before and After Surgery. Psychosomatic Medicine, 17: 428-454.

17.   Urban, W.H. "The Draw-A-Person Catalogue for Interpretation Analysis. Western Psychological Services. Los Angeles, 1963.